HABITATS OF THE WORLD

GRASSLANDS

Written and Illustrated by
Sheri Amsel

A LUCAS • EVANS BOOK

RSVP

RAINTREE
STECK-VAUGHN
PUBLISHERS
The Steck-Vaughn Company

Austin, Texas

For Peggy and Case Prime

Consultant: James G. Doherty, General Curator, Bronx Zoo, Bronx, New York

Book Design: M 'N O Production Services, Inc.

Library of Congress Cataloging-in-Publication Data

Amsel, Sheri.
    Grasslands / written and illustrated by Sheri Amsel.
      p.   cm. —— (Habitats of the world)
    "A Lucas/Evans book."
    Includes index.
    Summary: Discusses the world's grasslands and their animals and the need to conserve them.
    ISBN 0-8114-6302-8
      1. Grasslands—Juvenile literature.   2. Grassland fauna—Habitat— Juvenile literature. [1. Grasslands animals.   2. Grasslands.
    3. Prairies.]   I. Title.   II. Series: Amsel, Sheri. Habitats of the world.
    QH87.8.A48   1993
    574.909'53—dc20   92-8788
                                                                          CIP
                                                                          AC

Printed and bound in the United States.

1 2 3 4 5 6 7 8 9 0   VH   98 97 96 95 94 93

Table of Contents

GRASSLANDS OF THE WORLD

Imagine a sea of waving grasses. In some places the grass grows as tall as an elephant. In the distance, a great plain of this grass spreads out with only a few shrubs to be seen and a lonely grove of trees where a river cuts through. In this place it is too dry for trees, but too wet for desert plants. The grasslands of the world are found between the wet forests and the dry deserts.

Since there are few trees to nest or hide in, some of the larger animals survive by their speed. They are among the fastest animals of the world. Because danger can come from many directions, animals often travel together in herds.

Small animals make their homes in burrows here. In this way they are protected from the shadeless heat of the day, the cold of the night, and the hungry predators. Even raging grass fires do not threaten life underground.

The grasses can grow back even after animals graze on them or fires burn them. In their barren beauty, the grasslands seem indestructible.

The North American Prairie

The North American prairie covers much of the central and western part of the United States to the Rocky Mountains and spreads into northern Canada and down to Mexico. The wind always seems to blow. Years ago, before the white man began to "pioneer" the prairie, great herds of bison roamed the vast grassland. Their numbers were so great that the ground would tremble as they passed. Their constant grazing and trampling of the prairie kept the grass short. Whenever lightning started a prairie fire, it was limited. As soon as the fires had passed and the ground had cooled, new green stems began to shoot up.

Bison

As the railroad spread across the prairie, people shot millions of bison for their meat, for their hides, and just for sport. Their numbers fell at an alarming rate. By the end of the 1800s, the bison were almost extinct. As the bison disappeared, the prairie grasses grew long, and fires raged out of control more and more often. Many kinds of plants could no longer grow on the prairie. The Native Americans suffered greatly from the loss of food, clothing, and sources of shelter that the bison provided.

Some prairie life survived the pioneering of the plains, though the numbers of these animals will never be as great. Pronghorn antelope still graze in small herds. When they become startled or smell the approach of coyote or humans, the pronghorn use their great speed to race across the prairie to safety.

Huge prairie dog towns spread out, covering acres of grassland. Food for the black-footed ferrets, owls, and snakes, the prairie dogs were an important part of the grassland food chain. Pioneers began destroying prairie dog colonies to make room for farms and ranches. Later, fearful that their cattle and horses would break their legs in the abundant holes, they began poisoning the prairie dogs. As prairie dogs died off, the black-footed ferret began to disappear as well and is now thought to be extinct in the wild.

Owl

Pronghorn antelope

Prairie dog

Prairie chicken

Every spring on the grassland a strange and beautiful ritual begins: the courtship dances of the prairie chicken. At sunrise, the male prairie chicken dances and clucks, filling its bright orange air sacs to impress any females in the area. Sadly, prairie chicken numbers have greatly declined as the grasslands are plowed under for agriculture.

Rattlesnakes on the prairie eat insects and rodents and sleep away the winter in prairie dog dens.

Coyotes are another prairie predator. They eat rodents, birds, lizards, and domestic animals killed by winter hardships.

Coyote

Rattlesnake

Jackrabbits are also well suited for the grassy plain. Long ears allow them to hear danger from far off. In a flash they can speed away, covering ten feet with each jump.

But of all the animals of the American prairie, probably the most abundant and hardy will always be the prairie grasshopper. In a year when there is a grasshopper outbreak, they are blamed for millions of dollars in crop losses.

Jackrabbit

Prairie grasshopper

The African Veldt and Savanna

In Africa, the grasslands are called savannas and range from desert grass plains to those of trees and bushes. The veldt, typical of the interior of South Africa, is a vast area of treeless grassland. Together, this open country is home to many of the world's largest land animals.

Here the cheetah, said to be the fastest land animal in the world, chases a young zebra across a grassy plain. If the zebra can escape the cheetah's first blast of speed, it has a chance because the cheetah can run that quickly only for a short time.

Zebra

Cheetah

The lion hunts differently from the cheetah. Members of the pride work together to startle a herd of grazing animals. Pushed on by the stalking lions, the herd will move toward where lionesses lie in hiding to ambush an unlucky zebra or gazelle. When the animal is dead, the lions take turns feeding on it, guarding it while others in the pride rest or go off to drink.

Gazelle

Lion

Zebra

Vulture

Jackal

Hyena

Jackals and hyenas are mostly scavengers, that is, animals that feed on animals already dead. Waiting until the big cats have eaten their fill, the jackals and hyenas move in to eat what is left over. They may even scan the sky for circling vultures, other scavengers, that signal an animal nearby has died.

With few trees to slow them down, animals can run great distances on the veldt. The ostrich's seven-foot height and keen eyesight give it a great advantage in seeing predators from far off. If danger is spotted, its great speed takes it to safety.

Animals on the veldt often travel in large herds. The more there are to watch and to sniff the air for danger, the safer they are. That is why it is not unusual to see herds of ostriches, zebras, gazelles, and wildebeests traveling together. Living in groups is also a good way to search for food and teach the young.

Wildebeest

Zebra

Ostrich

Gazelle

The termite is one of Africa's smaller animals, but it builds its home so large that they can be seen all across the savanna. Out of clay and chewed grasses, they make towering nests as tall as a giraffe and as hard as a rock.

The dung beetle builds its round nest in the droppings of other animals. Then it lays its eggs inside. As the offspring develops, it eats its way out of the nest.

Out on the savanna, a thirsty elephant will tear apart a baobab tree to eat the spongy, moist inner wood.

Giraffe

Baobab tree

Dung beetle

Elephant

Termite

Harrier eagle

Secretary bird

Weaverbird

A common bird of the savanna is the weaverbird. Using long stems of grass, they weave great hanging nests. When many weaverbirds build their nests together, the construction can look like a haystack up in a tree.

On the ground the "secretary bird," named for its black-and-white suit and quill-like head feathers, hunts for mice and snakes to eat.

From above, the brown harrier eagle circles, scanning the hot African plain. As always, life here is a race to find food without becoming someone else's meal.

The Pampas and Llanos of South America

In Argentina, a flat, grassy plain, called the "pampas," spreads from the Atlantic Ocean to the Andes Mountains. Much of the pampas are dry and sandy. The areas that have water have been colonized by the people of Argentina. Still some of the natural grassland remains and, with it, some of the original animal life.

Burrowing owls hunt for insects, rodents, or birds. Then they retreat underground to sleep. Pampas deer and gray foxes also live on this grassy plain.

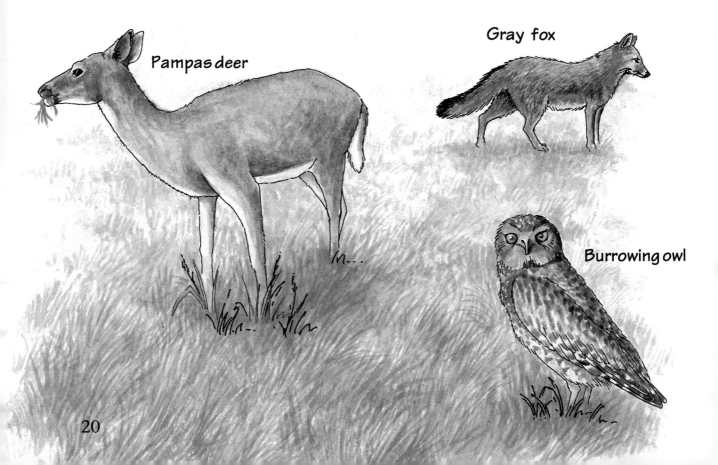

Pampas deer

Gray fox

Burrowing owl

Guanaco

Small herds of guanacos live in the wild here. They are perfectly suited for the pampas. Their long necks help them see danger coming, and they run so quickly across the rocky plains they are soon out of danger. Newborn guanacos are on their feet within fifteen minutes of birth, and within an hour they are speeding alongside their mothers.

A few herds of rhea, the South American ostrich-like bird, still roam the grasslands. One male bravely protects a group of females and their eggs from prowling foxes or skunks. He then goes on to raise the young! The rhea cannot fly and have been hunted for their meat, for their feathers, and for sport almost to extinction.

Rhea

South American savannas, found throughout Brazil, Colombia, and Argentina, are called "llanos" and change throughout the year. In winter they are dry, and fires often blacken the ground. But then in April the rainy season begins. Suddenly rivers swell, and the plains become flooded. They stay wet until fall.

Fox

Crocodiles and giant anacondas hunt the waters for prey. The anaconda can grow to over 20 feet long. The capybara, the largest rodent in the world, is well suited for the summer floods. It feeds on water plants and spends much of its time safely submerged in the water among greenery.

Brilliantly colored birds, like the scarlet ibis, also come to find refuge in the flooded plains. Where there is water, there is life.

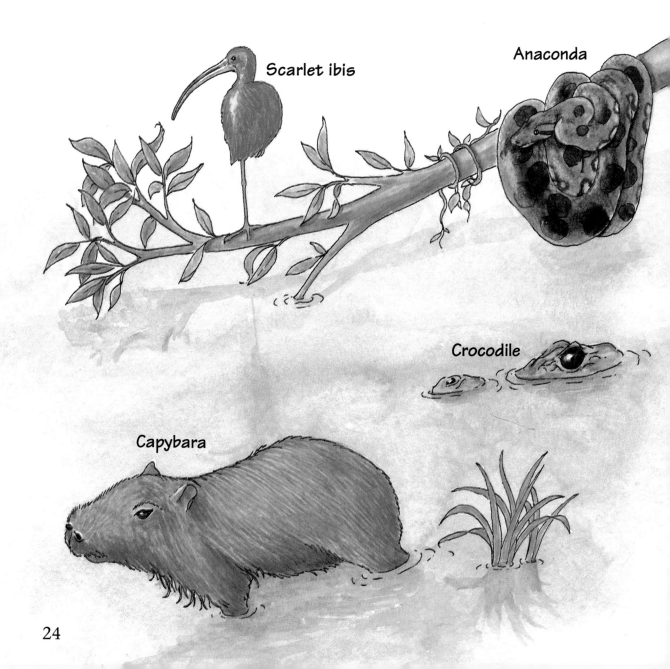

Scarlet ibis

Anaconda

Crocodile

Capybara

The Steppes of Central Asia

The grassland steppes of Eurasia spread from eastern China across Mongolia and Russia to Europe. The soil can be a rich, fertile black with tufted grasses, wild tulips, irises, and steppe thistles. Blue sage, camel's grass, and poppies all sprinkle the plain. A silvery sea of grass bending in the wind for much of the year, the grasslands finally turn yellow in the summer.

Poppy

Iris

Steppe thistle

Once herds of great tan horses, named after a Russian explorer Przewalski, roamed this land. But by the 1960s these horses could be found only in zoos.

Another rare sight on the grassland is the untamed bactrian camel.

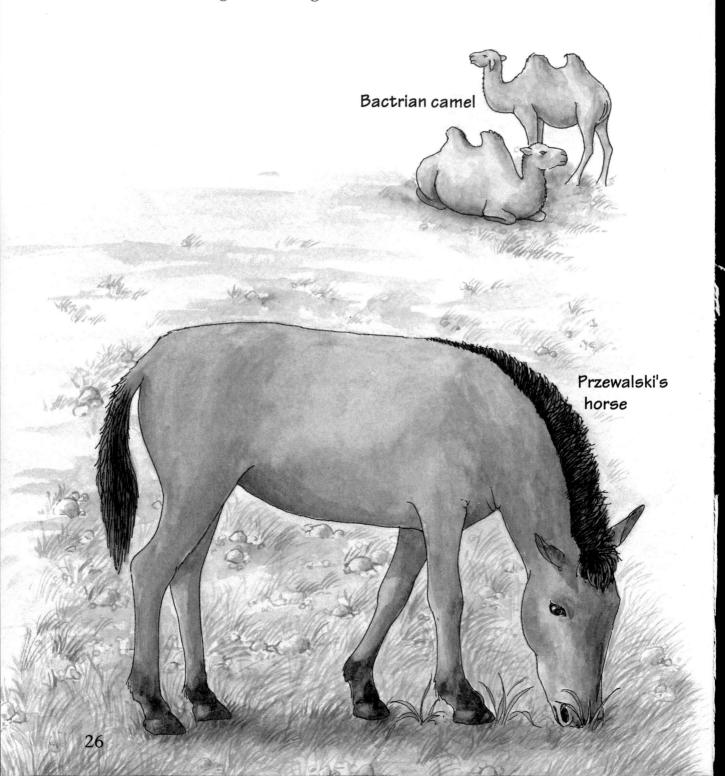

Bactrian camel

Przewalski's horse

Saiga

Sand grouse

Saiga also traveled in large herds, grazing on the plentiful grass. They are able to survive even in times of drought because of their ability to go for a long time without water. The saiga can endure the severe cold because of its strange snout that acts to warm and humidify the air. Once numbering in the millions, like the American bison, it was hunted and killed almost to the point of extinction. But luckily it eventually became legally protected and has now grown back to safer numbers.

Large colonies of sand grouse feed on grass seeds and are known to fly amazing distances in search of water.

Bobac marmot burrow large and complex communities on the steppes.

Long-legged bustards run along on the ground, living on insects and small animals. They have been heavily hunted because of their value as tasty game birds and have become scarce over much of their range.

The marbled polecat searches burrows for rodents to eat. Very much like a weasel, this little meat eater can be a fierce fighter, especially if its young are in danger.

On the steppes, it can be both fiercely cold and deathly dry. Only the most fit survive.

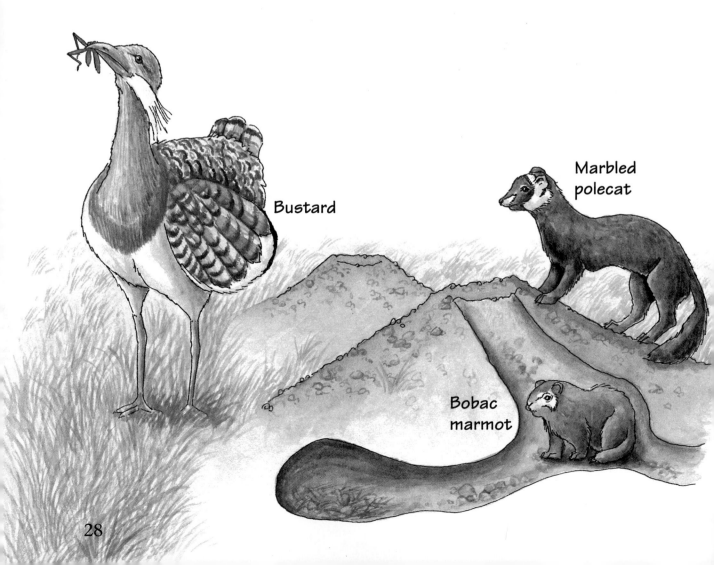

Bustard

Marbled polecat

Bobac marmot

Grasslands Today

All over the world, grasslands have provided the most fertile soil and richest grass cover. As farmers and ranchers have fenced and plowed these plains, the character of the grasslands has been changed forever. Farmed and grazed, the fertile topsoil is often washed or blown away. This once rich land then becomes more of a desert land, supporting less and less life.

In the United States small areas of tall grass prairie are carefully being replanted with as many of their original plants as possible. In Africa national parks have been set up to try to protect the dwindling wildlife that often competes with growing livestock needs. In the future, perhaps we can bring back and preserve the natural, rich treasures of the world's grasslands.

Glossary

burrow: a hole in the ground made by an animal

drought: a long spell of dry weather

extinct: no longer existing

food chain: the flow of energy as one animal consumes another

grazing: feeding on grass

herd: a group of one kind of animal living together

humidify: to put moisture into

pampa: a grassy plain in South America

pioneering: coming into a new area and making it more suitable for human inhabitants

plain: a large area of level or rolling treeless country

prairie: a broad tract of level or rolling grassland

predator: an animal that lives by killing and consuming other animals

prey: an animal taken for food by another

pride: a group of lions living together

ritual: a ceremonial act

rodent: any of a large group of small mammals with sharp front teeth used for gnawing

savanna: a grassland containing scattered trees

scavenger: an animal that eats dead animals or decaying organic matter

shrub: a low, woody plant or bush

steppes: an extensive plain, usually without trees, with wide temperature changes

Animals Index

Plants Index